THE 10 CUTEST ANIMALS

BY RACHEL ROSE

Minneapolis, Minnesota

Credits

Cover and title page, © Hung_Chung_Chih/Getty Images, © ALAN MORGAN PHOTOGRAPHY/Alamy Stock Photo, and © Matilda_Turner/Shutterstock; Title Page, © Hung_Chung_Chih/Getty Images; 4, © Yü Lan/Adobe Stock Photos; 5, © Dwi Yulianto/iStock; 6, © Danita Delimont/Alamy Stock Photo; 7, © Mike Hill/Getty Images; 8, © Daniel/Adobe Stock Photos; 8–9, © shane partridge/Alamy Stock Photo; 10–11, © Lauren Suryanata/Shutterstock; 12–13, © Philip Thurston/iStock and © Iva Dimova/Shutterstock; 14, © Danita Delimont/Adobe Stock Photos; 15, © Design Pics Inc/Alamy Stock Photo; 16, © Nature Addicts/Shutterstock; 16–17, © TERRY/Alamy Stock Photo; 18, © Andrew Nicholls/iStock and © wrangel/iStock; 19, © JIE GAO/iStock; 20, © Paul/Adobe Stock Photos; 20–21, © Photography Phor Phun/Shutterstock; 22T, © Callingcurlew23/iStock; 22M, © Kung_Mangkorn/iStock; 22B, © mattiaath/Adobe Stock Photos; 23, © Martin Pelanek/Shutterstock.

Bearport Publishing Company Product Development Team

Publisher: Jen Jenson; Director of Product Development: Spencer Brinker; Managing Editor: Allison Juda; Editor: Cole Nelson; Associate Editor: Naomi Reich; Associate Editor: Tiana Tran; Art Director: Colin O'Dea; Designer: Kim Jones; Designer: Kayla Eggert; Product Development Specialist: Owen Hamlin

Statement on Usage of Generative Artificial Intelligence

Bearport Publishing remains committed to publishing high-quality nonfiction books. Therefore, we restrict the use of generative AI to ensure accuracy of all text and visual components pertaining to a book's subject. See BearportPublishing.com for details.

Library of Congress Cataloging-in-Publication Data is available at www.loc.gov or upon request from the publisher.

ISBN: 979-8-89232-638-4 (hardcover)
ISBN: 979-8-89232-687-2 (ebook)

Copyright © 2025 Bearport Publishing Company. All rights reserved. No part of this publication may be reproduced in whole or in part, stored in any retrieval system, or transmitted in any form or by any means, electronic, mechanical, photocopying, recording, or otherwise, without written permission from the publisher.

For more information, write to Bearport Publishing, 5357 Penn Avenue South, Minneapolis, MN 55419.

CONTENTS

Cutest of the Cute 4
#10 Gecko 5
#9 Emperor Penguin 6
#8 Koala 8
#7 Jerboa 10
#6 Axolotl 12
#5 Sea Otter 14
#4 Quokka 16
#3 Fennec Fox 18
#2 Giant Panda 19
#1 Meerkat 20

Even More Cute Animals 22
Glossary 23
Index 24
Read More 24
Learn More Online 24
About the Author 24

CUTEST OF THE CUTE

There are millions of **species** of animals in the world. They come in all shapes, colors, and sizes. Some are deadly, some are smart, and some are gross. But there are also a lot of animals that are just plain adorable!

WHAT ARE THE WILD WORLD'S 10 CUTEST CREATURES?

Read on to decide for yourself. . . .

#10 GECKO

Which critters have big, round eyes and darting tongues? Geckos! These little lizards use their tongues to smell the world around them and catch tasty insects. Special toe pads help geckos stick almost anywhere. They can scurry up tree bark and some are believed to be fast enough to run across water. *Zoom!*

These lizards make chirping and clicking sounds.

Geckos can detach their tails to escape from **predators**.

Geckos don't have eyelids. They lick their eyes clean!

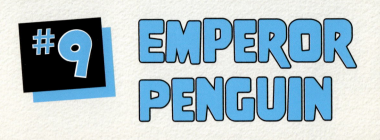

#9 EMPEROR PENGUIN

Brr! Emperor penguins live in some pretty chilly places. Luckily, they have found many ways to stay warm . . . and how they do it also looks adorable. These birds huddle together to block the freezing wind. Male penguins tuck eggs and tiny chicks under their bellies to keep them extra toasty. Anyone want to join the penguin pile?

These penguins dance! They flap their wings and sway to find a **mate**.

Emperor penguins also sing to find their mate.

#8 KOALA

Look up! Koalas may live *Down Under*, but these Australian cuties hang out up high. They spend most of their waking—and sleeping—hours in trees. Koalas can snooze in the branches for up to 20 hours a day. Baby koalas, called joeys, spend their tree time snuggled inside their mothers' pouches or clinging to their backs.

Koalas have two thumbs on each of their front paws.

Newborn joeys are the size of a jellybean!

These furry creatures can grow between 24 and 33 inches (60 and 85 cm) long.

Koalas eat about 28 ounces (800 g) of eucalyptus (*yoo-kuh-LIP-tuhs*) leaves every day.

#7 JERBOA

Boing, boing, boing! What's that hopping through the desert? Jerboas are tiny, strange, and totally cute. With their long back legs and even longer tails, these tiny **rodents** can leap up to 10 feet (3 m) off the ground. Their odd-looking ears work in adorable ways. Jerboas flap their big, floppy ears to keep themselves nice and cool in the desert heat. Who needs a fan?

A jerboa's tail can be twice as long as its body.

#6 AXOLOTL

Don't want to grow up? Neither do axolotls! They remain exactly the same as when they were born. While other **amphibians** lose their gills and move from water onto land, axolotls keep their cute, frilly gills and live their whole lives in a wet, underwater world.

Axolotls can make their skin lighter or darker to **blend** in with their surroundings.

#5 SEA OTTER

What's that floating pack of fluff? It's a group of sleeping otters! The furry animals stick together for life in the water. When snoozing, sea otters often hold hands and wrap kelp around themselves. This keeps them from drifting away as they rest. Awake or asleep, sea otters spend most of their time on their backs.

A sea otter uses its belly as a tray while it opens and feasts on clams and mussels.

These furry cuties can store food in pouches of skin under their armpits.

#4 QUOKKA

Say cheese! Because of their big smiles, quokkas are called the happiest animals in the world. But they're not actually smiling—it's just the shape of their faces and the way their front teeth stick out. Still, adoring visitors flock to the Australian island of Rottnest to take selfies with these camera-ready cuties.

These furry animals sleep curled up with their heads on their feet.

Quokkas hop to get around.

They can climb trees up to 7 ft. (2 m) high.

#3 FENNEC FOX

What's the cutest thing about fennec foxes? It's their enormous ears! These desert dwellers use their big ears to listen for faraway prey—even hearing critters that are underground! Fennec foxes can weigh up to 3 lbs. (1 kg). That's about the same as a toaster! There's a lot to love about the tiniest foxes in the world.

Pointy ears keep them cool during hot desert nights.

Furry feet help these foxes walk across hot, sandy deserts.

Don't be fooled by a fennec fox's button nose. Behind it are fierce teeth.

18

#2 GIANT PANDA

Giant pandas are one of the most adorable kinds of bears. These black-and-white cuties have round faces, big eyes, and playful personalities. Pandas often sleep on their backs with their legs up in the air! When they're awake, these bears can spend up to 16 hours a day munching on their favorite food—bamboo.

A long wrist bone helps pandas grasp bamboo.

Pandas poop as often as 40 times a day. They also sometimes pee upside down!

Baby pandas, called cubs, practice climbing on their moms.

#1 MEERKAT

Sleeping in a **burrow** at night can be cold. But once the sun is up, it's time for meerkats to warm up for the day. These cuties come out in groups ready to heat up under the sun. One of the ways they do this is by standing on their hind legs. Meerkats also lie on their backs for a quick sunbath!

Meerkats take turns babysitting all the pups in the family.

EVEN MORE CUTE ANIMALS

These 10 animals aren't the only cute faces in the wild. What others might make your heart melt?

HEDGEHOG
Hiding under all those prickly spines are cute furry faces. Hedgehogs roll into a ball to protect themselves from predators.

SLOTH
Like quokkas, sloths often look like they are smiling. They can hang upside down from trees for hours on end.

DOLPHIN
Dolphins use air to blow bubble rings underwater. Try popping these bubbles!

GLOSSARY

amphibians animals that have a backbone and live part of their lives in water and part on land

blend to mix in with

burrow a hole or tunnel that was dug by an animal to live in

forage to look for food in the wild

injured harmed or hurt

mate a partner chosen for having young

predators animals that hunt and kill other animals for food

rodents small mammals that have sharp front teeth

species groups that animals are divided into according to similar characteristics

waddle to walk in small steps, swaying from side to side

INDEX

Australia 8, 16
bamboo 19
burrows 20
desert 10, 18
gills 12
mate 6
mob 21
predators 5, 11, 22
prey 18
rodents 10
species 4
trees 5, 8, 16, 22

READ MORE

Johnson, Robin. *Animal Celebrities (Astonishing Animals).* New York: Crabtree Publishing Company, 2020.

Rose, Rachel. *Jerboa (Library of Awesome Animals).* Minneapolis: Bearport Publishing, 2025.

LEARN MORE ONLINE

1. Go to **FactSurfer.com** or scan the QR code below.
2. Enter "**10 Cutest Animals**" into the search box.
3. Click on the cover of this book to see a list of websites.

ABOUT THE AUTHOR

Rachel Rose writes books for kids and teaches yoga. Her favorite animal for all time is her dog, Sandy.